MAKING A PODCAST

BY NADIA HIGGINS

SEQUENCE

AMICUS | AMICUS INK

Sequence is published by Amicus and Amicus Ink
P.O. Box 1329, Mankato, MN 56002
www.amicuspublishing.us

Library of Congress Cataloging-in-Publication Data
Names: Higgins, Nadia, author.
Title: Making a podcast / by Nadia Higgins.
Description: Mankato, MN : Amicus/Amicus Ink, [2019] | Series: Sequence. Entertainment | Includes bibliographical references and index.
Identifiers: LCCN 2017049059 (print) | LCCN 2017049811 (ebook) | ISBN 9781681515243 (pdf) | ISBN 9781681514420 (library binding) | ISBN 9781681523620 (paperback)
Subjects: LCSH: Podcasting--Juvenile literature.
Classification: LCC TK5105.887 (ebook) | LCC TK5105.887 .H54 2019 (print) | DDC 006.7/876--dc23
LC record available at https://lccn.loc.gov/2017049059

Editor: Wendy Dieker
Designers: Ciara Beitlich and Veronica Scott
Photo Researcher: Holly Young

Photo Credits: sdecoret/Shutterstock cover; Forest Run/Shutterstock cover; Prostock-studio/Shutterstock 5; leezsnow/iStock/6-7; stray_cat/iStock 9; A. Aleksandravicius/Shutterstock 10; Nestor Rizhniak/Shutterstock 12-13; xijian/iStock 15; wavebreakmedia/Shutterstock 16-17; track5/iStock 19; Anthony Brown/Alamy 20; lechatnoir/Getty 22-23; Portrait Images Asia by Nonwarit/Shutterstock 25; andresr/iStock 26-27; Syda Productions/Shutterstock 29

Printed in China

HC 10 9 8 7 6 5 4 3 2 1
PB 10 9 8 7 6 5 4 3 2 1

TABLE OF CONTENTS

Radio on Demand

You just finished listening to a **podcast** on your tablet. Maybe this show was a mystery story. Or maybe it was a science lesson. Someone recorded this show and uploaded it to the Internet. Listeners download it and listen to it anytime. It's like radio on demand. It takes months to make a podcast, but it starts with one idea.

There is a podcast on every topic. What do you like to listen to?

LOADING... LOADING... LOADING.

OADING . . . LOADING . . . LOADING . . .

Podcasting equipment can be basic. Almost anyone can record a show.

Decide to make a podcast.

MONTH 1

. . LOADING . . . LOADING .

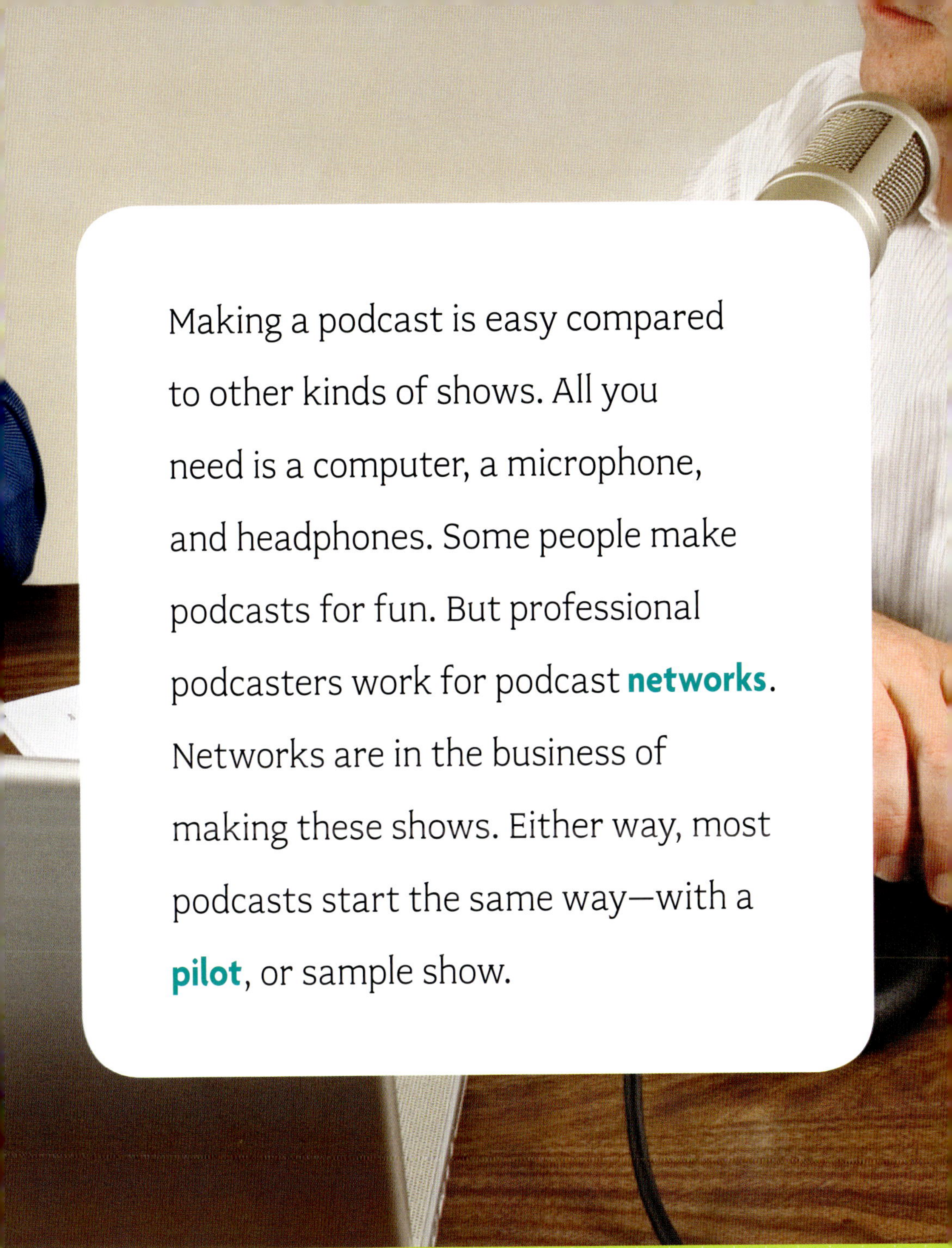

Making a podcast is easy compared to other kinds of shows. All you need is a computer, a microphone, and headphones. Some people make podcasts for fun. But professional podcasters work for podcast **networks**. Networks are in the business of making these shows. Either way, most podcasts start the same way—with a **pilot**, or sample show.

Often, a pilot idea begins with some questions. *What am I good at? What do I love? What do I want to talk about?* The answer might be a favorite TV show. A sport. Jokes. Clothes. Animals. Music. Books. Stories. There are real podcasts on all these topics. A curious person started a show about something they cared about.

What stories do you want to share? Podcasters start by thinking about what they like to talk about.

Decide to make a podcast.

MONTH 1 →

...LOADING... LOADING.

Pick a podcast topic.

OADING . . . LOADING . . . LOADING . . .

Every baker has had a kitchen disaster or two. Maybe those stories would make a good podcast.

Decide to make a podcast.

Write the pilot's script or outline.

MONTH 1 → MONTH 2 . . . LOADING . . .

Pick a podcast topic.

Planning It Out

Imagine a show called *Baking 9-1-1*. It is about baking disasters. This podcast takes a lot of planning. It will have a few **segments**. One segment will be an **interview** with a baker. Another will be some jokes about food. Does this show need a word-for-word **script**? Or is an outline good enough? The podcast writers make a decision and start writing.

OADING . . . LOADING . . . LOADING . . .

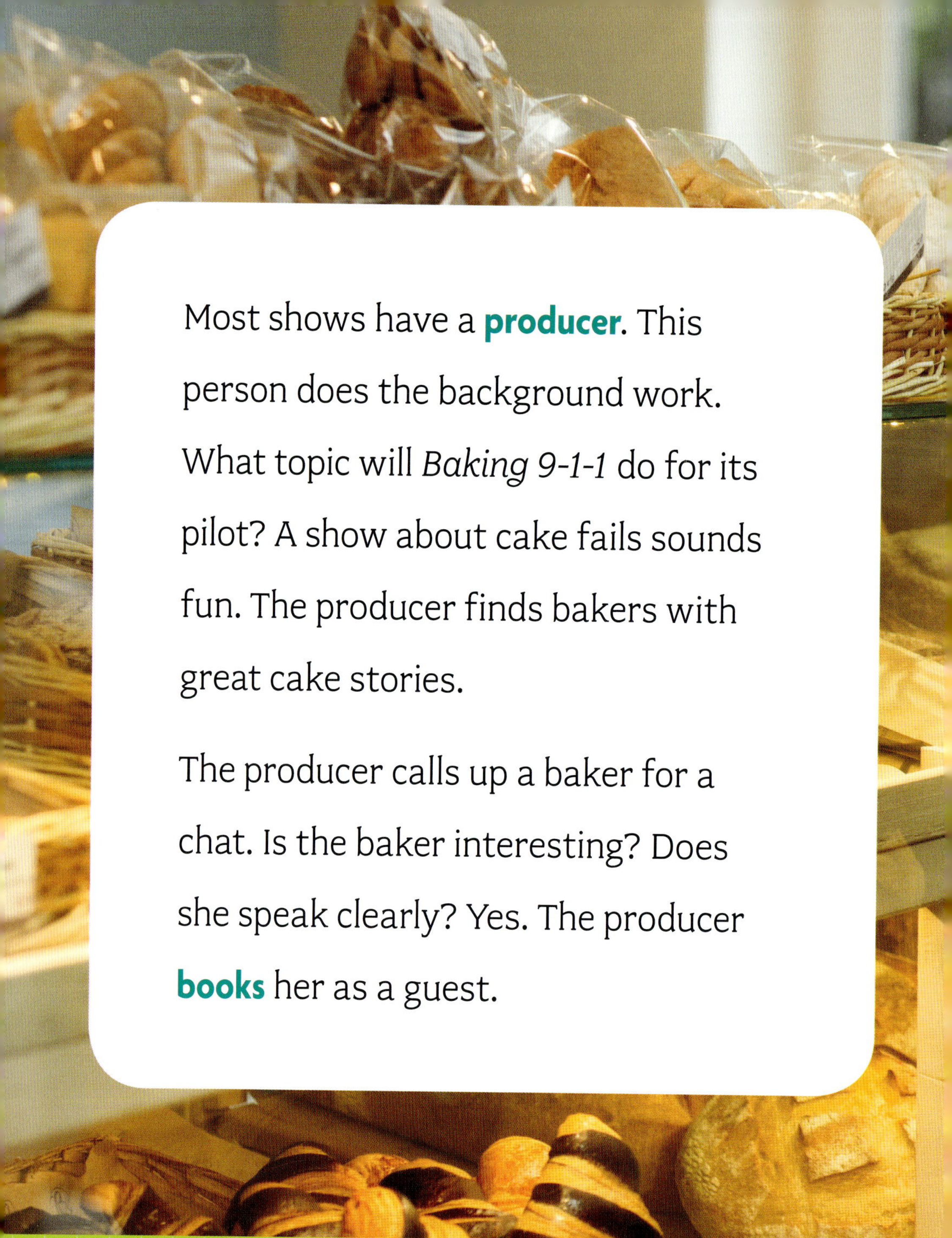

Most shows have a **producer**. This person does the background work. What topic will *Baking 9-1-1* do for its pilot? A show about cake fails sounds fun. The producer finds bakers with great cake stories.

The producer calls up a baker for a chat. Is the baker interesting? Does she speak clearly? Yes. The producer **books** her as a guest.

MONTH 1 → MONTH 2 →

- Decide to make a podcast.
- Pick a podcast topic.
- Write the pilot's script or outline.
- **Do research and book guests.**

Does this baker have a good story for the podcast? The producer will find out.

OADING . . . LOADING . . . LOADING . . .

Press Record

It's time to start recording the pilot. Each segment will be recorded separately. The **host** will start by recording a greeting. Next comes an interview. The guest lives in another city, so the host will do that interview over the phone. The show ends with jokes. Later, the segments will be put together in order.

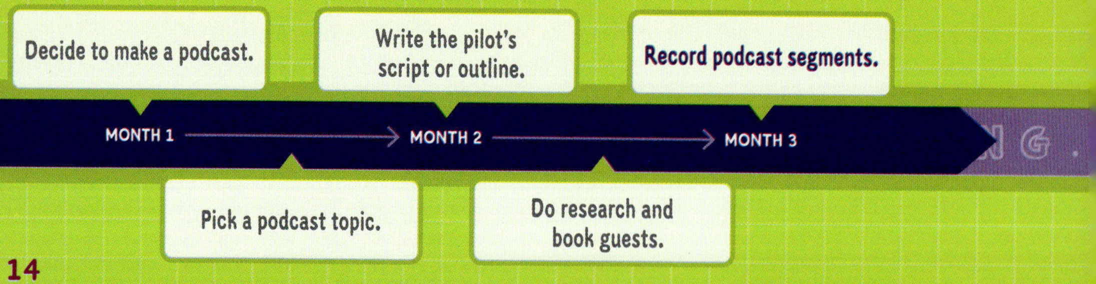

The host records segments for the podcast.

OADING . . . LOADING . . . LOADING . . .

Decide to make a podcast.

MONTH 1

Pick a podcast topic.

Write the pilot's script or outline.

MONTH 2

Do research and book guests.

Record podcast segments.

MONTH 3

The taping location matters. A professional **recording studio** is best. This special room shuts out background noise. But the guest is calling in from home. The producer wants her voice to be as clear as possible. The guest should call from inside a full closet. That reduces echoes and shuts out noise. The recording will sound much better.

A professional recording studio has lots of equipment that help recordings sound great.

The guest is a little nervous. The host helps her relax. The host asks great questions. But the guest fumbles her words. That's OK. The host starts the question over. The guest gets a chance to answer again. Only the best parts of the recording will be used in the show.

Recording an interview outdoors can help add interest for the listener.

Decide to make a podcast.

MONTH 1 →

Pick a podcast topic.

Write the pilot's script or outline.

MONTH 2 →

Do research and book guests.

Record podcast segments.

MONTH 3 →

Record guest interviews.

OADING . . . LOADING . . . LOADING . . .

A computer shows the sounds as waves along a line. The editor can see where voices begin and end.

MONTH 1
- Decide to make a podcast.
- Pick a podcast topic.

MONTH 2
- Write the pilot's script or outline.
- Do research and book guests.

MONTH 3
- Record podcast segments.
- Record guest interviews.

Putting It All Together

Recording is done. Now the **editor** gets to work. Editors put the pilot together. They cut out pauses and mistakes. They choose the best parts. They put the show in order.

The show has changed a little from the script. One joke fell flat. That gets cut. The interview went really well. It will run a little longer.

Edit interview and jokes; put segments in order.

MONTH 4

At last the first show is in place. The jokes are tight. The interview sounds smart. It is time to add **sound effects**. *Plop! Ding! Gasp!* These sounds make the show more interesting.

A composer wrote music just for the show. The editor mixes that in too. They check the levels. Are any parts too loud or too soft?

- Decide to make a podcast.
- MONTH 1
- Pick a podcast topic.
- Write the pilot's script or outline.
- MONTH 2
- Do research and book guests.
- Record podcast segments.
- MONTH 3
- Record guest interviews.

The sound editor adds in music and sound effects. This podcast episode is almost done.

Edit interview and jokes; put segments in order.

MONTH 4

NG . . . LOADING . . .

Add sound effects and music.

The First Episode

The pilot is done. Now what? At a podcast network, the bosses will have notes. They want different music. They want the show to be shorter.

Podcasters get lots of feedback. What works? What does not work? The podcast team makes another draft of the pilot. And another. With each draft, the show gets better.

Decide to make a podcast.

Write the pilot's script or outline.

Record podcast segments.

MONTH 1 → MONTH 2 → MONTH 3

Pick a podcast topic.

Do research and book guests.

Record guest interviews.

Podcast networks want their shows to stand out. They give notes on the pilot.

Edit interview and jokes; put segments in order.

MONTH 4

Add sound effects and music.

MONTH 5

Make more revisions of the pilot.

LOADING . . .

- Decide to make a podcast.
- MONTH 1
- Pick a podcast topic.
- Write the pilot's script or outline.
- MONTH 2
- Do research and book guests.
- Record podcast segments.
- MONTH 3
- Record guest interviews.

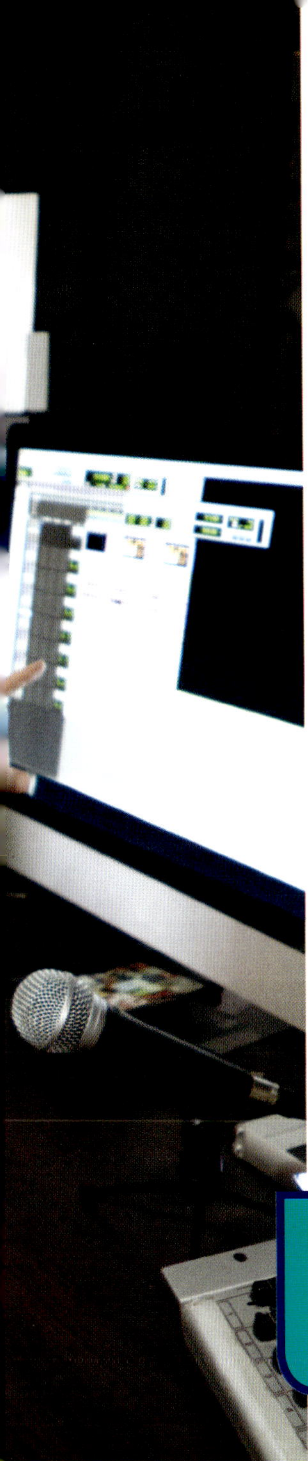

The first episode is *almost* ready to post online. Why is the team waiting so long? They want to make sure the format feels just right. Listeners do not like it when a show changes too much. The team also needs to figure out how long it takes to make each show. Once they know the final format, they decide to do one episode a month.

The podcast team works hard to finalize the details of the show.

MONTH 4
- Edit interview and jokes; put segments in order.
- Add sound effects and music.

MONTH 5
- Make more revisions of the pilot.
- Finalize the format and schedule.

ING . . .

The big day is here. Episode 1 goes up. Good news! Listeners are leaving five-star ratings. As the months go by, each episode picks up more listeners.

Fans email the show with comments. One fan has a great idea for the next show. The team decides to try it out. They are always on the lookout for fresh ideas.

A listener subscribes to the podcast. She doesn't want to miss the new episodes.

Decide to make a podcast.

Write the pilot's script or outline.

Record podcast segments.

MONTH 1 → MONTH 2 → MONTH 3

Pick a podcast topic.

Do research and book guests.

Record guest interviews.

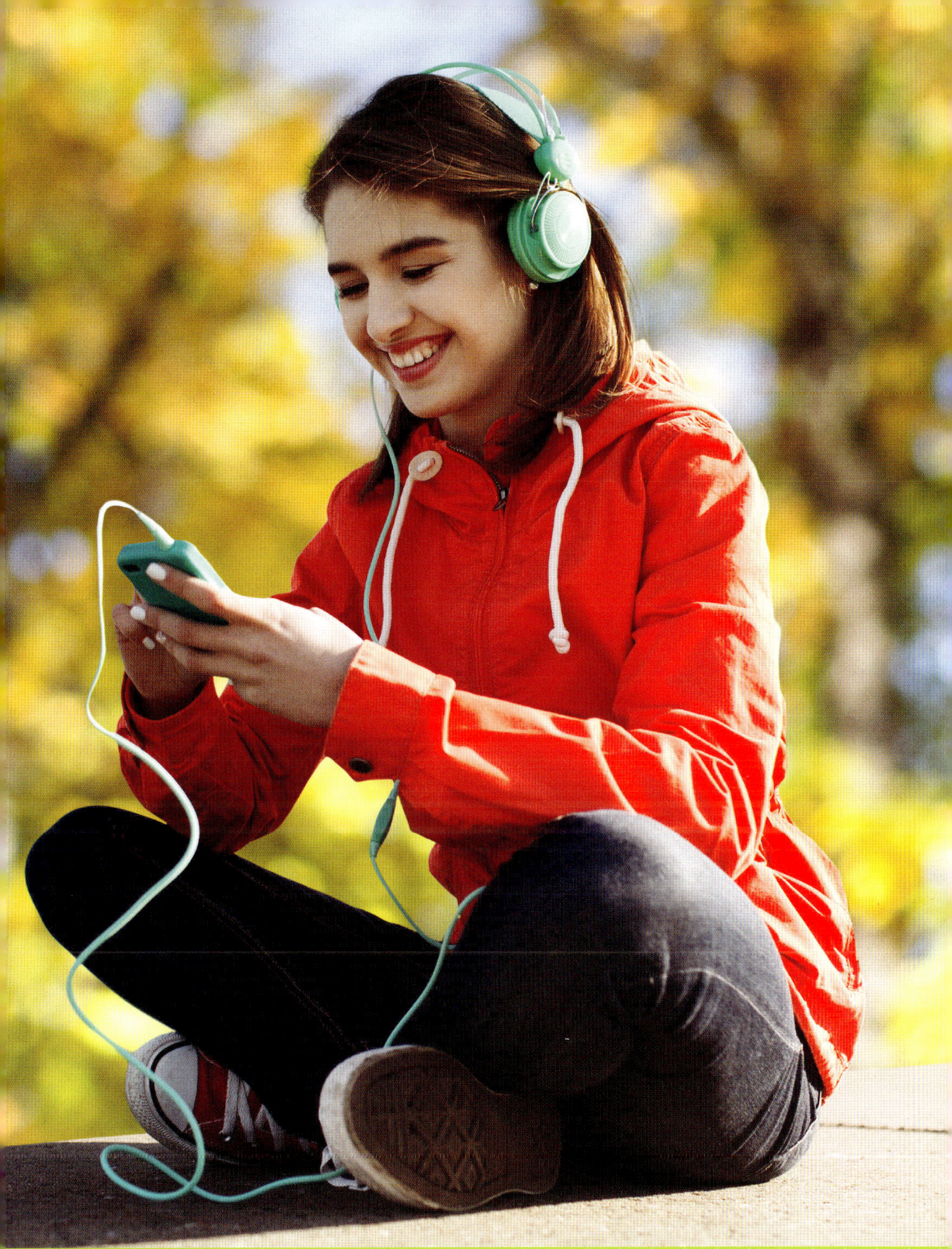

Edit interview and jokes; put segments in order.

Add sound effects and music.

Make more revisions of the pilot.

Finalize the format and schedule.

Post first podcast episode online.

MONTH 4 → MONTH 5 → MONTH 6

GLOSSARY

book To make an appointment with a person.

editor The person in charge of choosing the parts of the show that work best and flow smoothly together.

host A person who leads show segments and interviews guests.

interview To ask someone questions in order to learn more about a topic or person.

network A company that makes and promotes podcasts.

pilot A sample show that podcasters send to the network.

podcast An audio show, similar to a radio show, posted on the internet; podcasts usually have several episodes.

producer Someone who works behind the scenes to prepare for a podcast by finding guests, finding locations, and doing other tasks.

recording studio A soundproof room where people can record segments of a podcast.

script The words of a show written out word-for-word.

segment A standard part or section of a show, such as an interview.

sound effect A piece of sound, such as footsteps or blowing wind, that is added to a show after it has been taped.

READ MORE

Anniss, Matt. *Create Your Own Podcast.* Chicago: Heinemann-Raintree, 2017.

Fontichiaro, Kristin. *Speak Out! Making Podcasts and Other Audio Recordings.* Ann Arbor, Mich.: Cherry Lake, 2013.

Truesdell, Ann. *Fire Away: Asking Great Interview Questions.* Ann Arbor, Mich.: Cherry Lake, 2013.

WEBSITES

Common Sense Media: Best Podcast Apps and Websites for Students

https://www.commonsense.org/education/top-picks/best-podcast-apps-and-websites-for-students

NPR: Podcasts for Kids and Family

http://www.npr.org/podcasts/2036/kids-family

Scholastic.com: How to Conduct a Journalistic Interview

https://www.scholastic.com/teachers/articles/teaching-content/how-conduct-journalistic-interview/

INDEX

ABOUT THE AUTHOR

Nadia Higgins has been editing and writing books for 20 years. She has published more than 100 books for kids and teens. Nadia's favorite part of the job is doing research. She uses all kinds of media, from TV shows to podcasts, to find the best facts for her books.